15 Days of Prayer
With Johannes Tauler

Also in the *15 Days of Prayer* collection:

15 DAYS OF PRAYER
WITH
Johannes Tauler

ANDRÉ PINET

Translated by Victoria Hébert and Denis Sabourin

Liguori
LIGUORI, MISSOURI

Published by Liguori Publications
Liguori, Missouri
http://www.liguori.org

This book is a translation of *Prier 15 Jours Avec Jean Tauler,*
published by Nouvelle Cité, 1990, Montrouge, France.

Library of Congress Cataloging-in-Publication Data

Pinet, André.
    [Prier 15 Jours avec Jean Tauler. English]
    15 days of prayer with Johannes Tauler / André Pinet ; translated
by Victoria Hébert and Denis Sabourin. — 1st English ed.
        p. cm.
    Includes bibliographical references.
    ISBN 0-7648-0653-X (pbk.)
    1. Tauler, Johannes, ca. 1300–1361—Meditations. 2. Spiritual
life—Catholic Church. I. Title: Fifteen days of prayer with Johannes
Tauler. II. Title.

BV5095.T3 P5213   2000
269'.6—dc21   00–060571

Printed in the United States of America
04 03 02 01 00   5 4 3 2 1
First English Edition 2000

Table of Contents

How to Use This Book

AN OLD CHINESE PROVERB, or at least what I am able to recall of what is supposed to be an old Chinese proverb, goes something like this: "Even a journey of a thousand miles begins with a single step." When you think about it, the truth of the proverb is obvious. It is impossible to begin any project, let alone a journey, without taking the first step. I think it might also be true, although I cannot recall if another Chinese proverb says it, "that the first step is often the hardest." Or, as someone else once observed, "the distance between a thought and the corresponding action needed to implement the idea takes the most energy." I don't know who shared that perception with me but I am certain it was not an old Chinese master!

With this ancient proverbial wisdom, and the not-so-ancient wisdom of an unknown contemporary sage still fresh, we move from proverbs to presumptions. How do these relate to the task before us?

I am presuming that if you are reading this introduction it is because you are contemplating a journey. My presumption is that you are preparing for a spiritual journey and that you have taken at least some of the first steps necessary to prepare for this journey. I also presume, and please

excuse me if I am making too many presumptions, that in
your preparation for the spiritual journey you have determined that you need a guide. From deep within the recesses
of your deepest self, there was something that called you to
consider Johannes Tauler as a potential companion. If my presumptions are correct, may I congratulate you on this decision? I think you have made a wise choice, a choice that can
be confirmed by yet another source of wisdom, the wisdom
that comes from practical experience.

Even an informal poll of experienced travelers will reveal a common opinion; it is very difficult to travel alone.
Some might observe that it is even foolish. Still others may
be even stronger in their opinion and go so far as to insist
that it is necessary to have a guide, especially when you are
traveling into uncharted waters and into territory that you
have not yet experienced. I am of the personal opinion that
a traveling companion is welcome under all circumstances.
The thought of traveling alone, to some exciting destination without someone to share the journey with does not
capture my imagination or channel my enthusiasm. However, with that being noted, what is simply a matter of preference on the normal journey becomes a matter of necessity
when a person embarks on a spiritual journey.

The spiritual journey, which can be the most challeng-
ing of all journeys, is experienced best with a guide, a companion, or at the very least, a friend in whom you have
placed your trust. This observation is not a preference or
an opinion but rather an established spiritual necessity. All
of the great saints with whom I am familiar had a spiritual
director or a confessor who journeyed with them. Admit-
tedly, at times the saint might well have traveled far beyond

the experience of their guide and companion but more often than not they would return to their director and reflect on their experience. Understood in this sense, the director and companion provided a valuable contribution and necessary resource.

When I was learning how to pray (a necessity for anyone who desires to be a full-time and public "religious person"), the community of men that I belong to gave me a great gift. Between my second and third year in college, I was given a one-year sabbatical, with all expenses paid and all of my personal needs met. This period of time was called novitiate. I was officially designated as a novice, a beginner in the spiritual journey, and I was assigned a "master," a person who was willing to lead me. In addition to the master, I was provided with every imaginable book and any other resource that I could possibly need. Even with all that I was provided, I did not learn how to pray because of the books and the unlimited resources, rather it was the master, the companion who was the key to the experience.

One day, after about three months of reading, of quiet and solitude, and of practicing all of the methods and descriptions of prayer that were available to me, the master called. "Put away the books, forget the method, and just listen." We went into a room, became quiet, and tried to recall the presence of God, and then, the master simply prayed out loud and permitted me to listen to his prayer. As he prayed, he revealed his hopes, his dreams, his struggles, his successes, and most of all, his relationship with God. I discovered as I listened that his prayer was deeply intimate but most of all it was self-revealing. As I learned about him, I was led through his life experience to the place where God dwells. At that moment I was able to understand a little bit about what I was supposed to do if I really wanted to pray.

The dynamic of what happened when the master called, invited me to listen, and then revealed his innermost self to me as he communicated with God in prayer, was important. It wasn't so much that the master was trying to reveal to me what needed to be said; he was not inviting me to pray with the same words that he used, but rather that he was trying to bring me to that place within myself where prayer becomes possible. That place, a place of intimacy and of self-awareness, was a necessary stop on the journey and it was a place that I needed to be led to. I could not have easily discovered it on my own.

The purpose of the volume that you hold in your hand is to lead you, over a period of fifteen days or, maybe more realistically, fifteen prayer periods, to a place where prayer is possible. If you already have a regular experience and practice of prayer, perhaps this volume can help lead you to a deeper place, a more intimate relationship with the Lord.

It is important to note that the purpose of this book is not to lead you to a better relationship with Johannes Tauler, your spiritual companion. Although your companion will invite you to share some of their deepest and most intimate thoughts, your companion is doing so only to bring you to that place where God dwells. After all, the true measurement of a companion for the journey is that they bring you to the place where you need to be, and then they step back, out of the picture. A guide who brings you to the desired destination and then sticks around is a very unwelcome guest!

Many times I have found myself attracted to a particular idea or method for accomplishing a task, only to discover that what seemed to be inviting and helpful possessed too many details. All of my energy went to the mastery of the details and I soon lost my enthusiasm. In each instance, the book that seemed so promising ended up on my bookshelf, gathering dust. I can assure you, it is not our intention that this book end up in your bookcase, filled with promise, but unable to deliver.

There are three simple rules that need to be followed in order to use this book with a measure of satisfaction.

Place: It is important that you choose a place for reading that provides the necessary atmosphere for reflection and that does not allow for too many distractions. Whatever place you choose needs to be comfortable, have the necessary lighting, and, finally, have a sense of "welcoming" about it. You need to be able to look forward to the experience of the journey. Don't travel steerage if you know you will be more comfortable in first class and if the choice is realistic for you. On the other hand, if first class is a distraction and you feel more comfortable and more yourself in steerage, then it is in steerage that you belong.

My favorite place is an overstuffed and comfortable chair in my bedroom. There is a light over my shoulder, and the chair reclines if I feel a need to recline. Once in a while, I get lucky and the sun comes through my window and bathes the entire room in light. I have other options and other places that are available to me but this is the place that I prefer.

Time: Choose a time during the day when you are most alert and when you are most receptive to reflection, meditation, and prayer. The time that you choose is an essential component. If you are a morning person, for example, you should choose a time that is in the morning. If you are more alert in the afternoon, choose an afternoon time slot; and if evening is your preference, then by all means choose the evening. Try to avoid "peak" periods in your daily routine when you know that you might be disturbed. The time that you choose needs to be your time and needs to work for you.

It is also important that you choose how much time you will spend with your companion each day. For some it will be possible to set aside enough time in order to read and reflect on all the material that is offered for a given day. For others, it might not be possible to devote one time to the suggested material for the day, so the prayer period may need to be extended for two, three, or even more sessions. It is not important how long it takes you; it is only important that it works for you and that you remain committed to that which is possible.

For myself I have found that fifteen minutes in the early morning, while I am still in my robe and pajamas and before my morning coffee, and even before I prepare myself for the day, is the best time. No one expects to see me or to interact with me because I have not yet "announced" the fact that I am awake or even on the move. However, once someone hears me in the bathroom, then my window of opportunity is gone. It is therefore important to me that I use the time that I have identified when it is available to me.

Freedom: It may seem strange to suggest that freedom is the third necessary ingredient, but I have discovered that it is most important. By freedom I understand a certain "stance toward life," a "permission to be myself and to be gentle and understanding of who I am." I am constantly amazed at how the human person so easily sets himself or herself up for disappointment and perceived failure. We so easily make judgments about ourselves and our actions and our choices, and very often those judgments are negative, and not at all helpful.

For instance, what does it really matter if I have chosen a place and a time, and I have missed both the place and the time for three days in a row? What does it matter if I have chosen, in that twilight time before I am completely awake and still a little sleepy, to roll over and to sleep for fifteen minutes more? Does it mean that I am not serious about the journey, that I really don't want to pray, that I am just fooling myself when I say that my prayer time is important to me? Perhaps, but I prefer to believe that it simply means that I am tired and I just wanted a little more sleep. It doesn't mean anything more than that. However, if I make it mean more than that, then I can become discouraged, frustrated, and put myself into a state where I might more easily give up. "What's the use? I might as well forget all about it."

The same sense of freedom applies to the reading and the praying of this text. If I do not find the introduction to each day helpful, I don't need to read it. If I find the questions for reflection at the end of the appointed day repetitive, then I should choose to close the book and go my own way. Even if I discover that the reflection offered for the day is not the one that I prefer and that the one for the next day seems more inviting, then by all means, go on to the one for the next day.

That's it! If you apply these simple rules to your journey you should receive the maximum benefit and you will soon find yourself at your destination. But be prepared to be surprised. If you have never been on a spiritual journey you should know that the "travel brochures" and the other descriptions that you might have heard are nothing compared to the real thing. There is so much more than you can imagine.

A final prayer of blessing suggests itself:

> Lord, catch me off guard today.
> Surprise me with some moment of beauty
>   or pain
> So that at least for the moment
> I may be startled into seeing that you are
>   here in all your splendor,
> Always and everywhere,
> Barely hidden,
> Beneath,
> Beyond,
> Within this life I breathe.
>
> —*Frederick Buechner*

REV. THOMAS M. SANTA, CSsR
LIGUORI, MISSOURI
FEAST OF THE PRESENTATION, 1999

A Brief Chronology of Johannes Tauler's Life

JOHANNES TAULER IS ONE of the greatest mystics and preachers of the Middle Ages. His message has traveled across time and space and from person to person because of its essence and appeal. Yet, this man of many words never put his thoughts down on paper; his numerous sermons (all eighty of them) are his only legacy. And these seem to have been laboriously recorded by nuns as they were spoken, or from memory at a later date.

Tauler's statements are innovative, yet filled with the wisdom of his predecessors. He speaks of humility and simplicity (much like Saint Thomas) with a gentle and easy tone, using common sense and a directness which brings a breath of "fresh air" to his thoughts.

He praises silence and stillness as ways to find God within ourselves, to be one with Him, yet emphasizes action to spread the Word; we must use all of our faculties in order to reach Him. All of this makes him become a spiritual leader who transcends all man-made barriers, a modern thinker from a not-so-modern era.

HIS LIFE

Who was Johannes Tauler? What do we know about the man who seemed to know everything? Not very much, it seems...there are many gaps left to fill! Dates for what we do know are mostly approximations.

Johannes Tauler is presumed to have been born around 1300, in Strasbourg, a border city between three countries (France, Germany, and Switzerland). He was the son of a well-known and prosperous family.

Around the year 1315, he entered the Dominican novitiate in his hometown; at that time, it is believed that he was a student of Meister Eckhart, who had begun to teach there in 1312. His theological education is said to have been adequate to make him a "trustworthy" spiritual leader.

Circa 1325, it is believed that he attended the University in Cologne, where he met Henry Suso, who would become a lifelong friend, and Meister Eckhart, whose teachings and thinking influenced both of them.

Circa 1329, certain "outrageous" comments made by Eckhart were condemned by Pope John XXII, which prompted Tauler to step back and reflect upon his entire religious education, vow to avoid theological excesses and, most importantly, re-orient his life. From this, he decided to change the direction of his life from one of contemplation to one of action as a preacher. He left school.

In 1339, political conflicts forced Tauler and his Dominican brothers to leave Strasbourg for Basel; where he and Suso became the leaders of a large "society," the "Friends of God." This society, regrouping both religious and lay people, became a popular mystical movement which had as its objective the cultivation of holiness.

In either 1347 or 1348, Tauler returned to Strasbourg, where he began to preach; yet, as legend has it, lived the life of a hermit for two years following a series of controversial sermons. This legend has, itself, been the subject of numerous controversies. When he first returned to preaching, during his first sermon, it is said that forty persons were so taken with him and what he had to say that they went into convulsions and another twelve could barely be revived.

From approximately 1350 to 1360, Tauler returned to preaching in and around Cologne.

In 1360, Tauler made his final journey to Strasbourg, where he is reported to have died on June 16, 1361.

Introduction

No, the word is very near to you; it is in your mouth
and in your heart for you to observe (Deut 30:14).

Faithful to this oracle of the Old Testament, Tauler did not
seek God either in heaven or beyond the oceans, but in the
very deepest part of himself, in the "depth" of his soul. He
sought him with his "fundamental will," that is, with all of
his heart, soul, and all of his strength.

This God that he meets there is none other that the Word
of God, always being born within him, just as he was born
in Bethlehem, one Christmas Eve. We will also, upon following this preacher from Strasbourg, seek and meet God
at the very depth of ourselves.

This search for God will not progress without en-
countering various obstacles, for God will not allow himself to be caught easily and, above all, human nature,
distorted by sin, does not usually take the paths where it
is liable to meet him.

But God comes to help us. Even before we invoke him,
he is there! His grace makes us embark upon this path-
way, makes us follow it and takes us to its final end.

Because God loves us, we advance towards our meeting

as the father before his prodigal son. Jesus wants us to share the glory that he has near his Father and, to this end, sends us his consoling Spirit.

Our fifteen days together will unfold in the following manner: a contemplation on the birth of the Word of God within us (days one, two, three, and four); a wrenching away of ourselves and our egoism (days five, six, seven, and eight); for an offering of ourselves to God so that we can allow him to take over our beings (days nine, ten, eleven, and twelve); to live within us, making us participate in his divine life (days thirteen, fourteen, and fifteen).

Abbreviations Used in This Book

S (1, 7)   Sermon (number 1, paragraph 7) in the translation done by Huguenay, Thery, and Corin.

15 Days of Prayer
With Johannes Tauler

DAY ONE

The Birth of the Word in Us As in Mary

FOCUS POINT

Mary has intervened in human history, in the history of salvation. By the grace of God, and by Mary's own free will and acceptance of God's salvific plan, the Garden of Eden has been reclaimed for mankind through Jesus Christ. It is *through* Mary that the Father sends his divine Son, and it is *by* Mary that Jesus (in the flesh) is nourished in the womb, delivered into this world, and raised by a loving mother.

On the night that the Son of God was born of Mary, he became our brother. For eternity, he was engendered with-

1

out a mother, and through time, without a father. Saint
Augustine told us: "Mary was happier that God had been
born spiritually in her soul than the fact that he was born
of her flesh." Therefore, whoever wants to have this noble
and spiritual birth take place in his soul, as it did in Mary's
soul, must consider that these were Mary's special feelings,
that she was, at the same time, both God's corporal as well
as spiritual mother (S 1, 7).

Tauler invites us to contemplate on the three births of
the Son of God that occurred on Christmas Eve. First,
the eternal generation of the Word in the Holy Trinity is
evoked; then the birth of Jesus in Bethlehem, which Tauler,
following Christian tradition, considers to be a "birth without a father," as opposed to the eternal generation of the
Word, which is said to be "without a mother." Finally, the
daily birth of the Word of God in the depth of our soul
which will, by far, be the one treated at greatest length in
this Christmas Sermon.

Since Tauler invites us to do it, let us then contemplate on Mary, the mother of Jesus and our own mother,
as well as our model. May the Holy Spirit be our spiritual master.

Today, on the feast of the Immaculate Conception,
we celebrate the purity of the Virgin Mary's birth.
Through her, we have regained what had been lost
in the Garden of Eden. Now, all of the members of
the Mystical Body are regenerated through a return

to their origin. God, in his infinite mercy, by her, wanted to rescue us from the eternal abyss into which we had been thrown (S 55, 1).

In the fourteenth century, the dogma of the Immaculate Conception was not clearly defined and the matter remained somewhat open to discussion: Tauler, just like Saint Thomas, professes this truth. The description given that Mary was born pure, without sin and holy, does not allow us to determine whether Tauler thought that Mary was protected from sin or whether she was purified of sin between her conception and birth. Must we understand that the Word "sanctified" means purified, made holy, or exclusively as meaning filled with grace? Regardless, Mary was the first to benefit from the redemptive grace of her son.

Mary was a woman, our sister, and—through the part she played in our salvation—our own Mother. Since she was declared the Mother of God (according to the Council of Ephesus in 431), this fact authorizes the preacher to speak in the broadest sense of the phrase "Divine Virgin" even if it isn't quite theologically correct. In order to save the world (flesh), "the Word became flesh"; to save humanity, God became a man; but to destroy sin, he was not made sinful, even if the expression can be found in the Scriptures. He carried the sins of the world, he was consumed by them, but he did not personally commit them. Likewise, the Word of God protected his Mother from all aspects of sin in light of her exceptional role.

In the Church, Mary is a very special person, with a primordial and unequaled role. In the Old Testament, we see that women participated in the salvation of the Chosen

People (for example, Judith and Esther). In the same way, in the New Testament, a woman also intervenes in the history of salvation: Mary. Tauler underlines this for us with the phrase: "Through her, we have regained what had been lost in the Garden of Eden."

Mary does not regain our salvation; only God does. Let us be careful to neither maximize nor minimize her role. Christ is the only Redeemer. If we absolutely hold on to the idea and speak of Mary as a Co-Redeemer, let us note the subordinate character of this function: Mary is not redemptive "beside" Jesus but "below" him, as a servant of the Lord, being free to decide whether or not she would participate in his work.

In order to show Mary's role in Redemption, Tauler used the phrases "through her" and "by her." The first leads us to see, in Mary, a place where humanity can meet the noble image that had been lost. In fact, it was in the womb of the Virgin Mary that humanity, for the first time, would find God's image again. Our Eastern brothers express this mystery in a magnificent way in icons showing Mary, carrying in her womb, Christ in the image of the Father. According to the Litanies of the Virgin, Mary is called the "throne of wisdom." "Through her," that is, her womb, the wisdom of God, the incarnation of the second Person of the divine Trinity, the Son, is born. She carried the Bread of Life and, as well, gave birth to Jesus, the head of the Mystical Body of Christ as well as its body, that is, the Church. Through her, each of us has a place in the Church because we are members of the Body of Christ.

"By her": "God, in his infinite mercy, by her, wanted to rescue us from the eternal abyss into which we had been thrown." Mary's role was to assist, on behalf of humanity, in our rescue from the abyss of the sins committed in the Garden of Eden. Redemption passed through her; by using her, God made man take part in his own redemption. Her welcome of God's will into her life includes all our welcomes to God.

> This is what we read on the subject of the Virgin in the Book of Wisdom: "Come to me, all of you who desire me, and be filled with my birth." These words pertain to the heavenly Father. They lead us to the knowledge that comes from him, but they also pertain to the Blessed Virgin, for the same birth that takes place in the womb of the heavenly Father also belongs to her (S 55, 1).

The initial biblical reference refers to the Vulgate version of the Book of Wisdom (24:26). That is the wisdom of God that speaks; Tauler knows it and starts by following the strict tradition by applying those words to the heavenly Father. His comprehension of the words, "be filled with my birth," brings him to think of the eternal generation of the Word of God in the Holy Trinity and then from there he goes on to the birth of the Word of God incarnate in Bethlehem. That birth belongs to Mary. Christian tradition would lead us to bring these words to Mary and allow her to utter them to mean "be filled with the One I gave birth to," that is, Jesus Christ. God's wisdom as well as Mary, the throne of that wisdom, call us, not to draw us to her, but to her divine Son.

But Tauler doesn't stop there; he goes on to say: "the

same birth that takes place through eternity in the womb of the heavenly Father also belongs to her." His audacity surprises us, but faith confirms his words.

By looking at it from the point of view of the fruit of the birth, Tauler unites the two generations—the one of the Word within the Holy Trinity and that of the one through Mary—the first is eternal, the other temporal; the first totally divine and spiritual, the second is human and corporal. And Tauler speaks of the same birth! This generation finds its conclusion in the Person of Jesus. The heavenly Father eternally engenders his Son, and Mary, in a temporal sense, gives birth to Jesus in Bethlehem. The Person of Jesus is the Son of God. He was not conceived in a human sense, but was conceived by Mary through the Holy Spirit. From Mary, he received his human nature, but without sin. Born on Christmas Eve, he is equally man and God. The two generations come to the same fruition: the Person of the Son of God.

> *May the Holy Spirit make us enter the*
> *pure heart of Mary so that we may marvel*
> *before the sole human creature who never*
> *knew the darkness of sin.*
> *Mary, Mother of God,*
> *Give us your Son.*

REFLECTION QUESTIONS

How often do I incorporate Mary into my daily prayers? Do I see a need in my life for the intercession of her prayers? What different types of Marian prayers are available to me through the Church's rich tradition? What types of resources might I consult to find these prayer methods? Might I inquire at my parish rectory or with my spiritual director as to how I can strengthen my prayer life through Mary?

DAY TWO

The First Two Births of the Word

FOCUS POINT

God is one in his essence, but three in his Persons. God the Son processes from God the Father; the Father engenders the Son. The Son proclaims the Word of the Father here on earth, to us. The Holy Spirit is that deep love between the Father and the Son that rushes forth from the divine essence. The Incarnation (as Tauler says) is the "first birth." The "second birth" is the chaste and virgin Mary's "yes" to God's will, allowing the divine plan to be made manifest and be born from her body.

Today (Christmas) the Church celebrates three births, each one is a source of joy and delight for us so much that we should burst from jubilation, love, and recognition…. The first and most sublime birth is that of the only Son engendered by the heavenly Father in the divine Essence, in the distinction of the Persons. The second birth celebrated today is that which was fulfilled by a mother who, in her fruitfulness, kept the absolute purity of her virginal chastity. The third is the one by which God, every day and at all times, is truly born spiritually by grace and love into a good soul (S 1, 1).

Tauler treats three Christian mysteries: the first two will constitute our meditation for this day (the Holy Trinity and the Birth of Jesus), the third will be for Day Three.

The mystery of the Holy Trinity is evoked in the first place by the eternal birth of the only Son in the womb of God, one in three Persons. Then it is the incarnation of this Son, taking on the flesh of the Blessed Virgin Mary, in order to come and live amongst us. Our own sanctification is evoked by the birth of this same Jesus Christ at the deepest depth of our souls. God is alive and true. An excessive monotheism could easily lead to the concept of a "dead" God or at least one who is "still" because then there would only be one, no tension, movement, or life. God is one in his nature and divine essence, but three in his Persons, equal and divine.

If man abandoned God, He didn't abandon sinful humanity, but just the opposite; he loved them all the way to sending his only Son, for all time, in order to save them: the Incarnation that happened only once for all time in Mary, in which the Word became flesh, but which still continues today in each of us, for all time, spiritually in all people.

Tauler did not like to speak about the eternal generation of the only Son in the womb of the Blessed Trinity. In Sermon 29, he did not hide his revulsion at speaking about such a mystery, even to the point of taking the side of the theologians, presumptively taking the risk, by reserving the task of defending the faith to the Doctors and bishops. He even forbids lay people from reflecting upon it too much (see S 28, 2).... But he still spoke to them about it:

> It is absolutely impossible, in all intelligence, to understand how the high and essential unity is a single unity in essence, but triple with respect to the Persons. That is, how the Persons are distinct from one another: how the Father engenders the Son, how the Son proceeds from the Father and yet remains in him, and how, from the knowledge that comes from himself, springs forth an inexplicable reflux of love which is the Holy Spirit. All of this flows back in an unutterable kind of pleasure of the Holy Trinity with itself and in the enjoyment that the Trinity has for itself and in an essential unity (S 29, 1).

In a few very intense lines, Tauler successively shows us the existence and the action of the Holy Trinity, its profound life. "It is absolutely impossible, in all intelligence, to understand...." That is true, but it is not forbidden to seek to understand and less again to reflect, pray, meditate, and contemplate the mystery with the help of the Holy Spirit and of the Church. A disciple of Meister Eckhart, Tauler naturally sets out from the notion of "one," for the unique God is one in the nature of his divine Essence. God is the All-Other, the only one who exists by himself, and by whom everything exists. That is the foundation of our Judeo-Christian faith (ever since the revelation to Abraham). But Christianity does not stop there; Jesus revealed to mankind the existence in God of his Father and the Spirit. That is a clear enough revelation to motivate the apostles to establish these three divine Persons on equal footing. It took the fledgling Church three centuries to establish who those divine Persons are and their relationships to each other. Once he has established the unity of the nature and the Trinity of the Persons, Tauler speaks to us of their distinction and of their wonderful expressions of love. Between the Father and the Son, Tauler sees a relationship of generation (how the Father engenders the Son), of which he will describe the inverse—from the Son to the Father, that is, a relationship of procession, as opposed to one of generation, in which the Son proceeds from the Father. Here, the vocabulary must be carefully chosen, since faith does not accept all expressions. Thus, we can say that the Father "engenders" the Son since those are the words, "Father" and "Son," that Jesus used. We can also say that the Father "proclaims his Word"—an expression used by Saint John in the Prologue to the fourth Gospel. Then, in the same way, that "Son" and "Word" are synonyms, both designating the second divine Person, "generation" and "proclamation" designating a unique action.

When Tauler writes, "how the Son proceeds from the

Father and yet remains in him," all he really means is the equivalence of the two expressions, "engender the Son" and "conceive the Word." The second expression has the advantage that it shows the interiority of the act. The Son is always "in" the Father. Even after his incarnation, the Eternal Son never ceases to dwell in the Father.

We will complete this reflection with Tauler's words: "How this wonderful springing forth flows back [reflux] into the ineffable love of the Trinity itself." The words "flow" and "reflux" have great importance to Tauler. The flow runs from the unity of the divine Essence towards the Trinity of the Persons, passing through the divine nature which it renders prone to multiplicity. Inversely, the reflux flows back from the multiplicity of the Persons to the unity of the divine Essence. The Son's love for the Father will lead him to unite with his Father in the very depths of the unity of the divine Essence. There, and only there, the Son and the Father are truly one. That reflux is of concern to us since the incarnation of the Son has made us members of his Body, so that it is with us that he flows back to the Father in the divine Essence. But now we must speak of the second birth of the Son.

On that Christmas Eve, Jesus was born of Mary in Bethlehem. This event is part of history, for through his humanity Christ becomes a part of it, but he also transcends it, for his divine Person is far beyond our temporal limitations.

> Mary was a virgin, chaste and pure; she was a betrothed young woman; she kept herself apart from all that was going on around her when the angel came to her (S 1, 7).

This mystery of Christmas brings us back to that of the Incarnation, to the Annunciation, the moment when Mary's "yes" allowed God's plan to come to fruition. Following the teachings of Saint Augustine, Tauler compares this second birth to the first which he describes as a birth without a father, whereas he sees the other as a birth without a mother. In fact, in the eternal generation, the Son is conceived of the Father only, and at the Annunciation, only the mother is featured.

No one knows Mary's age at the time of the Annunciation. Tauler stresses that "Mary was a virgin, chaste and pure; she was a betrothed young woman." In Mary's virginity, Tauler discerns the double aspect of sterility and fertility: Mary is sterile in the eyes of the exterior world for which fertility was seen as the most important quality of a woman; but he also sees an interior spiritual fertility in her, which enabled her, according to the Christian tradition (and particularly to Saint Augustine), to spiritually engender the Word of God in her soul even before He was born from her womb.

Tauler follows the thinking of Saint Paul in his letter to the Ephesians: "Women, obey your husbands..." and saw, in the Annunciation, Mary's total submission to God as well as to Joseph, the first one encompassing the second. Mary had totally aligned her personal will with that of God. Finally, Mary had distanced herself from the world, more internally than externally, for she did not neglect either Joseph or those around her (the visit to her cousin Elizabeth proves this). But she remained very attentive to God's presence in her. In Tauler's words, Mary's fundamental will was constantly and totally concentrated upon the depth of her soul where God dwelled, just as her womb was the dwelling of the incarnate Word.

O Mary, the new ark of the Covenant,
Bearer of the Word of God incarnate
and of the Bread
Descended from Heaven.
Teach us to live
In the fertility of spiritual virginity,
And in total and joyful acceptance
of God's Will,
The source of the greatest freedom.

REFLECTION QUESTIONS

Do I often meditate on the mystery of Holy Trinity, the distinction of each Person of the Trinity, and the reality that each is singularly God in its essence? Which Person of the Trinity do I typically associate with authority? With friendship? With exuberance? With justice? With teaching? With forgiveness? Which person of the Trinity do I usually address in my prayer life? Do I feel drawn to vary this approach to the specific Persons of the Trinity in my prayer life from time to time, depending on the situation?

DAY THREE

The Birth of God Within Us

We must prepare a place for God in our hearts! We must clear our lives of those things less than God that tempt us to turn our lives away from God! Of course, all of this begins with God's grace, with God instilling in us the desire to seek him, to want him in our lives. Once we clear a space in our hearts—in our lives—for God, he will fill that space with his goodness, his peace, and his joy.

The third Mass is sung during the day, and it begins with these words: "A child is born to us, a son is given to us." It

represents this mysterious birth which must take place eve-
ry day, every instant, in good souls who prepare for it with
great care and sincere love. For we can only receive and feel
this birth in our inner self through regrouping all of our
strengths. In this birth, God belongs to us and gives himself
to us so completely that we can own nothing other than
him. This is what the passage means: "A child is born to us,
a son is given to us." He is, then, ours, totally and in every-
thing, for he is continuously engendered in us (S 1).

T he joy of a birth is greatly due to the eagerness of its
mother. Thus, we must ask ourselves if we genuinely
desire to have the Son of God born in us and dwell in our
souls. God's gift surpasses our request which is a prerequi-
site to it. Tauler often speaks of "a pure and simple intention to seek God" which seems to be a paradox. The purity
of the desire precludes all searches of our own initiative, all
"appropriation" of God, for God gives himself but doesn't
let himself be conquered. The simplicity of the heart stems
from unity. It is better to ask once from the bottom of
our heart than to launch many appeals that could be in-
terpreted as arrogance. Tauler speaks of a "sincere love,"
of a feeling that surpasses all feelings, a feeling which
springs from the superior faculties of the soul, affection
in as much as it is love, and intelligence in as much as it
is sincerity. Through them, the "depth of the soul" expresses itself in unutterable moans (using the words of
Saint Paul).

The author also speaks about a great care which invites

us to "tend towards," to lean us over this birth of God in us by faith, love, and hope, like a mother over the cradle.

Since Tauler compares this third birth of the Word to the second, let us ask what Mary's feelings were prior to and at the birth of Jesus, and let us pray to the Holy Spirit to place them within us.

In Sermon 24, Tauler describes the wait for the Holy Spirit. The comings of the Holy Spirit and of the Son of God within us are not without analogies, above all in that which concerns the preparation of our soul. We must make our preparations in much the same way as the farmer who has grafts to do to his trees in the spring: trimming, pruning, pulling out the weeds, turning and carefully working the soil. The allegory is clear when referring to our situations: pulling out weeds means to fight against the seven capital sins which are always present in us, at least in our tendencies to excesses. That is only the first step! "Cut and prune" is a task that is slower, more delicate and more exacting: the purification (exterior and interior) of our attachments. Our heart rivets itself to many things, legitimate or not, when it should be truly linked only to God. God does not ask that we break away from our legitimate attachments, but for their continuous purification: this is a long-winded project because a hard-won victory often makes us discover another battlefield where a new intervention awaits us. Psalm 42:7 says "Deep calls to deep": the discovery of God brings with it that of our misery; that is where hope plays a role. "Purify the exterior and the interior"— this advice had already been given by Jesus to his contemporaries: Tauler made a definite distinction between the exterior person and the interior or noble one. The first has not yet declared war on bad inclinations, while the second is already well engaged in the spiritual battle; but it too must "purify the interior," or, rather, let God purify it, for that is God's task. Our task is the preparation for the purification.

The farmer must "turn the soil," says Tauler (S 24, 2), and he also gives us the meaning of that term in the following comparison: thus man must take great care to search his soul, to scrutinize the innermost depths there, to redirect what has steered away from his goal in him (S 24, 2). "To search his soul" constitutes the main task of one's spiritual life. Another expression also describes the same spiritual action: to descend into oneself.

Such a descent is realized through faith, love, and trust: "a regrouping of all of our strengths" (S 1). Not an act of faith, charity, or trust, that regrouping is an attitude of the soul moved by desire, for we only obtain something if we desire it, and by putting intelligence and will into action. Thus, that regrouping could be defined as the love of the God we know or knowledge of the God we love. This regrouping is necessary for the birth of Word of God in us. It is not the source of it, but a condition for it.

Our contemplation brings about the coming of God. When we prepare a place for God in the depth of our soul in this manner, he fills it completely. Tauler has numerous thoughts on this:

> If you stay mute...he speaks! If you come out of yourself...he enters! If you void your soul...he fills it! What we want to achieve is to be his in the most perfect and elevated manner and give him all the

room he needs to operate and grow there without obstacles (S 1).

Thus, God hungers to give himself to us. The only obstacle would be to obstruct our soul by cluttering it with created things. If we want Christ to be born in us like he was in Mary, we must repeat after her: "A child is born to us, a son is given to us...." Through this birth, God is ours, God belongs to us like Jesus belonged to Mary. He is ours completely and everywhere for he is continuously engendered in us. Such is the gift of God to humanity—his own Son!

Our disbelief is also an obstacle to this gift and our faith is so weak!

> *May God grant us the grace*
> *To prepare our hearts for this birth*
> *And for this rest,*
> *so that he can be spiritually*
> *Born in us. Amen.*

REFLECTION QUESTIONS

In what way is God trying to be born within me? How do I respond to his divine plan? Do I clear out space in my heart so that he will fill me with his love? Am I ready to say "yes" to God at work within me, allowing him to shine through me even during those times when I am afraid or tired or angry? How do I feel spiritually when I refuse God in my life, when I say "no" to his divine plan? How do I go about reconciling with God after I have said "no" to him and later regret it deeply?

DAY FOUR

The Desire for God

FOCUS POINT

It is said that cognition precedes appetite, that we must first know something before we can desire it. In the case of God, to know him is to love him. The Holy Spirit graces us with the desire for God, and the more we know him (and we have known him from the first moment of our conscious existence), the more we desire him. The "virtuous cycle" continues: we are free to choose God; it is easier to choose God when we are free of those attachments that distract us from desiring him.

Where is the one who was just born, the king of the Jews? We want to adore him, to praise him, and honor him with myrrh, frankincense, and gold.

The soul knows that God exists, even in natural light, but what is he? Where is he? That is completely unknown to the soul and hidden from it; it knows nothing about it. But suddenly a loving desire awakens in the soul and forces the soul to seek answers, to try to learn what is hidden and veiled about God (S 4, 1).

D esire is the basis of life; without it, the soul dies. Many great desires at the most basic level drive humanity: our professional life, our affections, and those unimaginable efforts that we exert in order to survive the tough times prove their existence. Knowledge inspires desire and the media which dominate our era know it: to inform is to trigger desire. The natural knowledge of God awakens desire in us and, in as much as we identify God with peace and justice, we become ardent defenders of one and the other. The soul knows that God exists, even in natural light. Tauler does not linger on that natural knowledge of God since he is speaking to religious who are already under the influence of professed faith. All he wants to do is teach them the dialect of faith and supernatural desire.

God reveals himself and then hides: he makes himself felt to be close and then disappears. Thus, that is how he excites our desire for him. Where is he? Tauler replies: "Seek him at the very depth of your soul!"

Desire leads to knowledge. Between the two there is a two-way, cause-and-effect relationship: desire gives birth to knowledge which, in turn, spurs desire. One of our most common mistakes is to interrupt that virtuous circle.

The soul carefully informs itself just like the Magi did. We too must ask: "Have you seen him whom my soul loves?" (Song 3:3). Or again, "Where is the child who has been born king of the Jews?" (Mt 2:2). Desire requires a certain freedom: the same freedom that the Magi had with respect to their paganism, the same as a Christian with respect to his religious faith. The believer who is too attached to his worldly things will never be a seeker of God. Thus, we must be free, possessing our faith without being possessed by it.

The soul comes from God through creation while secondary human forces call it to generation. Thus, having come from God, the soul must return to God. It will accomplish that reflux through its desire for God which will, at first, be natural, then supernatural. That desire is a grace in as much as we ask for it and in that it fits into God's plan.

In its return to God, the soul must be the same as when it came from the hands of the Creator, that is, pure and immaculate, for God cannot create sin. Tauler does not deny the existence of the original sin, but he does not attribute this to God.

Since man sins essentially through an excessive attachment to worldly things, he can only be saved through his detachment from the disorder within him. Within the confines of both the infinite and the finite, man can only turn towards God by turning away from sin.

Preaching on the feast of the exaltation of the Holy Cross, Tauler commented on this passage from Saint John (12:32):

"And I, when I am lifted up from the earth, will draw all people to myself." This gives us a valuable example of what we just said, that is, we cannot, at the same time, look towards God and the world... (58, 1).

The beginning of the desire for God is both a conversion and a glance towards God. It is not that the world is bad or that we must flee from it, but it must remain in its proper place in our hearts. God remains the target of our affections. That desire must grow within us. Tauler cites many examples of this in Sermon 58.

In another of his sermons, Tauler links the desire for God to the Holy Spirit. Citing Saint John (7:37–38), "Let anyone who is thirsty come to me, and let the one who believes in me drink...," Tauler reflects upon this thirst and gives the following answer:

What is that thirst? It is simply this: when the Holy Spirit comes into a soul and lights a flame of love, it provokes a fire of love in it. From the flames of that fire come the sparks of love that kindle a thirst and delicious desire for God (S 11, 2).

Here we have, by far, passed beyond the natural desire for God, reaching the level of infused ardor, even beyond the theological virtues. According to Tauler, this desire stems from the Holy Spirit and its gifts, gifts which effectively link desire to its action in the soul. The goal of this desire is the heart of Christ.

The growth of the desire for God is linked to the Holy

Spirit. That is how God pursues mankind, which is a theme that is dear to Tauler as we find it in many of his sermons, in particular in Sermon 11.

At the end of this first part of this retreat, dedicated to the birth of the Word in us, let us look at Mary, a chaste and pure young woman, betrothed to Joseph and to God. In her, the Mother of God, the divine Word became flesh in order to live amongst us. Since then he is born in us at every instant, each time we desire him.

Virgin Mary,
Mother of God and Our Mother,
Intercede on our behalf to the Holy Spirit:
May he inflame our hearts with
an ardent desire for God
And may the Word dwell in us
In a perpetual birth.

REFLECTION QUESTIONS

Do I find that the more I know about God—the more I encounter him in my daily life—the more I desire to know him? Have I experienced this "virtuous cycle" in my life? What are those attachments in my life that sometimes hinder my choosing God? What steps can I take to remove such attachments from my life? If these attachments are not clear to me or if I do not know how to remove them from my life, might consulting with a spiritual director be beneficial to my spiritual life?

DAY FIVE

Temptation and the Enemies

FOCUS POINT

Every day we pray to God: "Lead us not into temptation." But when we inevitably encounter temptation in our lives, we are faced with a decision: submit to the temptation before us or choose the God who saves. Temptation can serve to strengthen our lives in God, for when we choose God rather than the temptation, we reaffirm our desire for God, and only God. External and internal temptations may assail us, but God's grace can overcome any and all temptations that may come our way.

It is by living through temptations that we come to know what rock bottom is. Temptations are quite useful, they become as profitable as virtues to whoever is willing to consider them as such. In the same way as grace is necessary, so is temptation. For it is in temptation that virtue is conceived and it is also how it is achieved. In order to become real, virtue must stand the test of temptation. In the same way, man will be tempted both internally and externally in all facets of life (S 75, 2).

S o, consider yourself warned! Temptation is waiting for you to step outside your door! It is useful and even indispensable—yet we must use it wisely. The Bible shows us many examples of temptation at work; sometimes more obvious than others.

Saint Paul said: "be strong in the Lord" (Eph 6:10). Tauler echoes this. It is up to us to practice it.

Tauler also distinguishes between internal and external temptations. Once you conquer the external ones, you still have to deal with the internal ones.

There remains, within you, a world over which you will not triumph without a great deal of effort and God's help. Within yourself, you will face three strong and determined enemies which you must defeat and who are rarely defeated (S 2, 3).

Leave the cloisters to the religious, just remember that the spiritual life requires a certain indispensable breaking away from the world. This break opens many hostilities with our internal enemies: vanity of the spirit, our own flesh, and Satan.

One who is vain wants to be noticed in all aspects of his life. Our flesh and the sensations it produces lead us to all manner of impurities. Satan is discussed at length by Tauler: attacking us by inspiriting all kinds of meanness, hate, revenge, and negative judgments against others. For Tauler, Satan is ever-present and constantly at work against us. Satan cannot act directly upon our will but tempts it through his deceitfulness.

Why must there be all those obstacles on our road to finding God? Why all of those renunciations and stripping bare which make us poorer, yet still do not apparently give us God? It is through temptations that we see rock bottom, we see the very depth of our soul in different ways.

Trials separate our true friends from others by showing the fidelity of one and the abandonment of the other. In the same way, temptation reveals the fidelity of our own heart. At the foot of the cross, the apostles were few—the cross will reveal our worth. The cross is also a dynamic of growth within us for good.

Tauler sees temptation as a grace: "In the same way as grace is necessary, so is temptation. For it is in temptation that virtue is conceived and it is also how it is achieved." No one will contest the necessity of grace, but many will the necessity of temptation. Man can choose to either accept or reject God. And his attitude often wavers between the two.

Finally, temptation introduces us to Christ:

> God can give himself just as well through tempta-
> tion as through virtue or the Holy Sacraments. It is
> through temptation that the stains and deep roots
> of sin are found and eliminated. It is through temp-
> tation that the fear of God engenders humility and
> that we are invited to seek shelter in him, and en-
> trust him to fight our battles (S 75, 2).

Tauler is audacious when he compares temptation to a sacrament, which is a gift from God and a place of meeting. A
temptation that is not defeated is a trap that closes around
us, and that is where humility comes into play. For temptation puts us in our proper place before God. When a Christian survives a trial, he attributes the victory to God. But
when he is defeated, he looks for Christ's benevolent glance,
just as Saint Peter did after his denial.

Our Father
Who art in heaven...
Lead us not
Into temptation...

REFLECTION QUESTIONS

What role does temptation play in my life? What attitude
do I adopt with respect to temptation when I encounter it
in my daily life? Do I approach temptation as a challenge, a
means of proving my love for God by overcoming the obstacle I see before me? How do I respond to failure in the

face of temptation? Do I "beat myself up" over a failure, or do I make it a point to rededicate myself to God with greater passion than before?

DAY SIX

Our Five Captivities

FOCUS POINT

Tauler brings to our attention five "captivities," five prisons, from which Christ has come to set us free. He frees us from our undue love for created things; he frees us from our love for our selves; he frees us from a spiritual arrogance that attributes those good things that come from God to ourselves; he frees us from loving those elements of worship (prayer, incense, ceremony) more than we love God; and he frees us from an attachment to our own will that prevents God from seeing his will at work in our lives.

"When he ascended on high he made captivity itself a captive" (Eph 4:8). There are five kinds of captivities in which

*people are imprisoned and which Christ eliminates when
he fulfills his ascension in us (S 19, 1).*

━━━━

Tauler explains to us what is that captivity which Christ
brought with him when he ascended into heaven. If
you jail the jail keepers, you free the prisoners. In the same
way, when Christ removes our bad tendencies, he removes
the demons and frees us.

> The first of our captivities consists in being a pris-
> oner of our love for created things, whether inert or
> living, each time that we do not love God through
> them (S 19, 1).

Tauler knows that God only created good. He knows that
God ordered man to cultivate the world. Tauler preaches
neither separation from nor spite for the world, but he wants
our love to conform to God's plan. If such is not the case,
then God, in his mercy, warns us through signs.

> It is a noble and good sign that they are not aban-
> doned by God, since God invites them and attracts
> them constantly, day and night.... The one who does
> not close his ears and who heeds the divine warn-
> ings, will be saved (S 19, 1).

At this point, the mistake is still slight. What Tauler insists
on is much more serious: our attitude towards the warn-
ings, because the future of our spiritual life depends on it.

> The second captivity consists in the fact that many
> fall in love with themselves. It is astonishing to see
> how they consider this love to be just and legitimate
> (S 19, 2).

A minimum of self-love is justified: a woman could dress
up nicely and think she is a beauty and a businessman think
he is indispensable! But an overabundance blocks all spiritual progression. Tauler exclaimed: "how difficult it is to
deliver them from their captivity!" In fact, the captivity tight-
ens: from the sensory realm, it passes to the will. For those
who accept that they have made a mistake, repairing it is
relatively easy, but if we refuse to admit it, we are lost. Our
obstinacy could become stubbornness and violence if we
believe that we are defending something that is good. There
are no worse wars than religious ones! Tauler can't find
harsh enough words to describe these persons: "these people
are no longer people, they are mad dogs, ferocious wolves"
(Ibid). Tauler then speaks of "angry words, the desire for
revenge, falsehoods, publishing things that should be kept
quiet…," a sorry sight of a person who is a captive of
self-love. The self is despicable because it is arrogant, the
mother of all vices.

Spiritual arrogance consists of appropriating for itself
the good that is within us instead of bringing it back to
God: that is the third captivity. Tauler shows us this:

> That is why there is a great difference between those
> who live according to the Scriptures and those who
> only study them. Those who only study them want
> to be highly thought of and honored; they put down

those who live them, holding them to be idiots, back-ward....

Whereas those who live them, they believe that they are sinners and are filled with mercy for others... (S 19, 3).

The division cited above, those who study the Scriptures and those who live them, is faulty because it ignores two additional groups: those who study the Scriptures and live them and those who ignore them completely. Tauler was never a spiritual "Master" and his audience was only comprised of religious, yet he was greatly appreciated.

His thoughts still ring true: wisdom tells us that we should blame ourselves for those bad things we find in ourselves and give God credit for the good. One form of arrogance consists of establishing one's own spiritual itinerary instead of receiving it from God.

The fourth captivity is surprising by its strangeness: "that of spiritual favors"! It is as if God's gift could hinder our path to him. The goal of favors is to accelerate it, but they could stop or suspend it.

Many stray by following him from too far away, by giving themselves to him without moderation, by seeking too much, and stopping excessively; for it appears to be a great good to which they abandon themselves that they possess in joy. But nature keeps its share, and it is only the joy that we harvest when we believe that we have grasped God (S 19, 4).

There is an error in discernment: prayer must be distinguished from the consolations one finds there. Neither the incense nor the music is God; to stop at either one is to put an end to our journey.

Must we then pray with a full soul whether God makes us feel his presence or his absence? Our prayer must be the same whether it is in the face of the Sun of Justice or the Dark Night.

Our reaction when those consolations end represents a criteria of discernment. Blessed is the one who, like Job, praises God in all circumstances.

> The fifth captivity is that of the will itself. Man wants to accomplish his own will even in things that are of God and in God.... I would by far prefer a man of perfect abandon who shows few accomplishments and of lesser appearance to a man who is eminent by his deeds and appearance and who would show less abandon (S 19, 5).

It is normal for man to sail his own boat! But his domination over the world is not left totally to his own free choice. Freedom consists in giving a filial "yes" to God's plan. For Tauler, "perfect abandon," although it may instill fear in some of us, is a trusting abandonment to God.

Most Holy Virgin Mary,
You who always said yes to God's plan,
Please intercede with your Son
So that his passion frees us
Of all undue attachments

And so that his mercy greets us
Free, reconciled, and filled with joy.

REFLECTION QUESTIONS

How aware am I of the "five captivities" in my life? Do one of these five prisons apply to my life more than the others? If Christ has freed me from these captivities, do I recognize that it is me who continues to imprison myself by choosing to live in the captivity of one of these five prisons? Do I recognize that each of these five attachments can be overcome by the grace of God? Am I ready to call upon God's grace in my life and seek the detachment and abandon that God calls me to pursue?

DAY SEVEN

Descend Into One's Own Depth

___

FOCUS POINT

God wants to reside within each one of us and, as has been mentioned previously, we must clear out a space within ourselves so that he will have that place he seeks. Of course, we are speaking of humility here. We are speaking of detachment from those things that tempt us and can control us if we do not keep ourselves spiritually fit. We must follow Jesus to the depths of our soul, clearing out what does not belong, freeing up space for the Lord. It is at these depths where the Word will take root and flourish within us.

G od wants to be born in you: we must have the desire
for it and prepare him a place by eliminating the obstacles. According to Tauler, we should descend into our
own depth or already be pursued there by God in order to
establish the order that is required for the birth of the Word
within us.

We have already made reference to Sermon 9 in previous chapters. Tauler insists on the theme of the descent into
one's self, to the depth of one's soul, into one's true depth.
Christ descended amongst us in order to save us; from a
divine condition, he assumed a human one, then one as a
slave, condemned to the cross. We must mystically follow
him in this "kenosis." The story in the Gospel of Saint
Matthew (15:21–28) about the Canaanite woman's faith
illustrates Tauler's theme: "Jesus left the district of Tyre and
Sidon..." (S 9, 1).

Tauler saw Jesus "descending" from Jerusalem, a place
where God was known, to Tyre and Sidon, pagan cities.
The Canaanite woman that he met will also be invited to
descend spiritually into her own depth. Having dared to
ask Jesus to free her daughter, who was being tormented by a
demon, she saw herself spurned by the silence of the Master.

The more Jesus spurned her, the more the woman
humbled herself: "It is a sigh that comes as if from an end-
less depth with no bottom" (S 9, 4), but that was only the
beginning. By descending into herself, she felt the necessity
to call to Christ from there, and the inattention he showed
towards her only accentuated her hope: "Oh, how at that
moment, from the depth, the desire must reach out, becom-
ing more urgent" (S 9, 5).

The Lord humbled her even more, comparing her to

dogs! That is where the second equal but different theme of the pursuit appears and comes into play. Jesus, by making the Canaanite woman descend into the deepest of her humility, pursued her:

> How could he have tempted her and tested her even more, pursued her and pressed her more closely? She allowed herself to be cornered and she pursued her very depth even deeper than he could pursue her. She pushed the hunt to the depth, she penetrated even deeper into the abyss by saying: no Lord, I am not even a dog, not even a little dog… (S 9, 5).

The two themes intermingle: the depth into which the soul must descend and the pursuit, all brought together by the word "dog."

God hunts for and pursues us in order to lead us to the very depth of ourselves, into this depth where the Word will be born.

Let us leave it to the reader to appreciate the mercy of the hunter (God) and look at what Tauler thinks. God would not permit us to be tempted beyond our limitations; to Simon Peter, Jesus said: "…Satan has demanded to sift all of you like wheat, but I have prayed for you that your own faith may not fail…" (Lk 22:31–32). Saint Paul replies, echoing this: "No testing has overtaken you that is not common to everyone. God is faithful, and he will not let you be tested beyond your strength, but with the testing he will also provide you the way out so that you may be able to endure it" (1 Cor 10:13).

The truce (end of your temptations when you can take

no more) does not have the negative tone that we see in it in the pursuit, but just the opposite, it shows God's tenderness: the goal of temptation is to make us desire God; if it is excessive, it will lead us to a denial, too weak, it would fail its goal. Experience provides examples of temptations that seem to be unsupportable; can we determine the terms? Only God is the judge of his requirements and man's replies.

Tauler attaches an important and even surprising consideration to this phrase. It seems that man, who is overextended, harassed, and at the end of his rope, can find, in an instant, a new youth, an ardor that was previously unknown through a divine favor. This permits him to get back onto his journey towards God, just as he was at the beginning.

Here, in a Pentecostal context, Tauler evokes the first coming of the Holy Spirit: gift of God, spiritual exhilaration, the accomplishment of miracles, and so on. That is really an inundation of the Holy Spirit!

In view of this gift from God, Tauler sees three possible reactions:

- A new spiritual life which is more ardent, more lively, and supported by the Holy Spirit and its charisma;
- Some might keep this gift secret in their hearts while being just as fulfilled as the others;
- An inability to support the great realizations of God in their soul for they are so powerful and great...death from a broken heart.

Tauler doesn't mention it, but those three reactions could be illustrated by the reactions of Saints Paul, John, and Thérèse of Lisieux.

Oh Spirit of the living God,
Come touch my heart.
Take me, guide me, in your love.
Come, Spirit of the living God,
Come touch my heart.

REFLECTION QUESTIONS

In what ways do I allow God to enter into my heart and guide me? Do I open up to him in service to others? In prayer? In nature? Do I plumb the depths of my soul, seeking out the darker corners and removing those distractions that prevent God from filling me up? Do I invite God's grace to aid in this reclamation of my soul or do I hide these darker corners from God and those closest to me? What (good) habits might I work into my life to increase my humility and longing for God?

DAY EIGHT

Only One Man Must Die

FOCUS POINT

Just as one man, Jesus Christ, died for the world, for the salvation of all, so must a part of each one of us die so that Christ might be alive in us. Our pride—our will—must die in each one of us. To others, it will seem as if we are lost, without direction, weak; in reality, we will be strong in the Lord by our own free will. He will guide us by his divine plan into the joy and peace of eternal life. Every time we fail while relying solely on ourselves is an opportunity to turn our lives over to God, the one who never fails us.

"[I]t is better for you to have one man die for the people than to have the whole nation destroyed..." (Jn 11:50). Saint John did not say these words on his own; the Holy Spirit was speaking through him. And that was his last prophecy before the death of our Lord. He also said: "this man is performing many signs. If we let him go on like this, everyone will believe in him, and the Romans will come and destroy both our holy place and our nation" (Jn 11:47–48) (S 14, 1).

T he Gospel of Saint John here speaks about the plot to kill Jesus where the high priest, Caiaphas, was the major proponent of putting Jesus to death in order to save the Jewish nation. Tauler ignores the historical context, touching only the spiritual one: this drama is played out in us today and we have the choice between the sacrifice of part of ourselves and our destruction. Jesus taught us that it was essential to renounce ourselves in order to follow him, and that only the grain of wheat that falls in the soil and dies will bear fruit. Tauler transposes this evangelic episode onto the moral and mystical level: our will must die in order to bring forth our union with God. Through faith, we know that Christ died for all mankind; so in this sense, the prophesy was true and it went beyond all expectations since not only the Jewish nation was being saved, but all of humanity was as well. The death of our self has no meaning unless it is united to the death and resurrection of Christ, the only source of sanctification.

Tauler gives three different calls from God to unite with him for our spiritual ascent:

For some, he calls them through public disgrace in order to keep the depth of their heart for himself, to awaken them and enlighten them internally (S 14, 1).

God could never be the author of disgrace, but can let something bad happen in order to preserve man's freedom and draw good from this negative situation: for example, Jesus was betrayed by his friends and rose from death to save the world. This reading of events requires a keen sense of God and of his teachings; God wants to keep the depth of our soul for himself. By saying that God wants to awaken us, Tauler echoes the biblical theme of the vigil and sleep (in the Garden of Gethsemane). He enlightens us internally by giving us a comprehension of God's plan. Jesus is the light of the world and shows the call from God in disgrace. Such is God's providence, to descend through humility and rise through love. Any mishap or strife can help us ascend.

If we die to our weaknesses, it will lead us to God:

God also draws some of us to him through penance...there is penance when we feel that we want to speak and yet we remain silent...when we detach ourselves from something that gives us pleasure while our senses tell us to hold on (S 14, 1).

In a time of laxity, such language would be considered masochistic! Tauler does not say to sever all ties, but only those that are excessive. His trilogy, "detach...turn away...release," highlights the excessive covetousness with which we grasp onto things and appropriate them for ourselves. Happy is the man who can see a flower, admire it, and continue on his way. He who picks it will see it wilt quickly. The spiritual life resides in that "turning away" from evil in order to see God's plan.

As for the third category, God attracts them by his own nature (S 14, 1).

We raise ourselves from the ethical level to the mystical one. God attracts us! Apparently the disgrace and penance are over. The spiritual life that is driven by the Holy Spirit is different from the one that results from our own efforts, even those that are helped by grace. It does not push the cross away but helps one carry it, it does not exempt one from death, but it gives love. The cross is then transformed, yet a man still has to die.

Tauler constantly brings back the presence of the cross and God's attraction. All of those detachments and penance are in vain and worthless unless they are impregnated with the love of God. He seeks salvation in the love that comes from God's heart.

In Tauler's eyes, to die to oneself is to give up great things in order to accomplish small ones with a great amount of love and humility.

Christ's death brought about the salvation of mankind, not through compensation, but through love. Jesus loved us to the point of dying for us. As for us, we must give up our own ideas and will in order to make them conform to that of Christ; that is, to change our opinion of things in order to adopt God's. And that is how we dive into the divine mercy. This opportunity is given to us at our baptism, through the holy sacraments and in prayer if we heed God's call. God expresses himself through life's upsets; they show a crack through which God's Word can enter.

Lord Jesus, you said:
"The One who has sent me is with me.
He has never left me alone,
Because I always do what pleases him."
Grant us your light so that we can discern,
In all things, the will of the Father
And the power of your love,
So that, having established it
We can fulfill it.

REFLECTION QUESTIONS

Are there times in my life where I try to do it all? Take on everybody and everything? Is it difficult to hand life over to the Lord when I think I have to be the one to see things through? Do I ever "let go and let God"? Why not? Do I think things would be out of control? Would I seem weak in the eyes of others? Would I seem less important in my own eyes? Perhaps I might feel freer and less anxious if I gave my life (especially the worrisome parts) over to God.

DAY NINE

God Is
at Work in Us

FOCUS POINT

We must humble ourselves so that God may fully enter us. Detachment is key in this spiritual process. We should not deny God's desire to enter into the very depths of our soul, nor our own desire (even though it might be screened by distraction) to have him there. We will find no rest until we rest in God and find God fully alive in our souls. Anything less than this and we will still desire more, until it is complete and full. We cannot be satisfied loving God anything less than completely.

God wants only one thing in the world, the only thing he needs, but he wants it so intensely that he gives it all of his attention. This is: to find man's heart empty and prepared to receive him so he can fulfill his divine work (S 5, 1).

W hen Mary was ready to give birth to Jesus in Bethlehem, she prepared the manger to receive the Word of God. It is up to us to prepare our soul and re-nounce ourselves, and trials help us do this. The time has come to let God do his work in us.

On the subject of this divine action, Tauler has diffi-culty expressing himself. We can think of two complemen-tary actions: he prepares the depth of our soul and then he dwells in it permanently. Tauler speaks of an immediate contact between the soul and God; through the virtues and the gifts of the Holy Spirit, God reveals and makes himself known and loved. Our experience with God, which is often underdeveloped, only needs to grow under his gaze. It can only be received from him. Knowledge of the mysteries is a gift from the Holy Spirit, wisdom, or the taste for God, is the greatest favor he can grant.

In order to further explain this concept, Tauler borrows the following comparison:

Take a basin that is filled with water and put a small mirror into it.... When the sun is at its highest, it will be seen in its entirety in the mirror, but only as a small disk (S 6, 3).

Leave it to the physicists for a technical explanation of this, but in spiritual terms, just like the sun is at the bottom of the basin, so is God at the depth of our soul. How can this be explained? How can the sun be in the mirror? How can God be in my soul? Is it just an image or is it real?

> When we place a screen, even a very small one, between the mirror and the sun, the sun completely disappears (Ibid).

Thus, it is an image. The image of God within us reminds us of the what was written in Genesis (1:26): "...he created mankind in our image, according to our likeness...." The importance of this analogy lies in the fact that Tauler borrowed it from Meister Eckhart and that Saint Teresa of Ávila took it up also in her autobiography.

Should we not go beyond the generally accepted meaning of the word "image"? In many instances, the Gospel reminds us that God will come to us, Father, Son, and Holy Spirit: "Those who love me will keep my word, and my Father will love them, and we will come to them and make our home with them" (Jn 14:23); or "...those who abide in love abide in God, and God abides in them" (1 Jn 4:16). Saint Paul himself said: "Anyone united to the Lord becomes one spirit with him" (1 Cor 6:17). All of those texts invite us to see more than an image in the soul, to see the living presence of God.

Tauler believes that for the common believer, God operates through images, and for others he acts directly.

Whereas we can pass scientific knowledge to one another, the knowledge of God must come directly from him.

Tauler speaks of God taking over the very depth of our soul, which for man corresponds to the total gift to God of what he has and what he is. It is not easy to let God prepare our very depth, for we are closely tied to our ideas, even with respect to sanctification. The ability to be able to accept everything from God is not achieved overnight.

What is essential in the spiritual life is to let God's sun penetrate our soul. That does not mean being passive, because God is Fire; he illuminates, burns, and consumes. In Tauler's eyes, this call from God is:

> An eternal attraction, and an inclination that is so powerful that even when man wants to ignore it, he finds no rest (S 6, 2).

Man is made for God and finds his true rest only in him. United with God, man descends into his mystery and feels the need to create a void, for he knows that God's all can only be received in that void (in man's soul).

> *Lord, make it so that I am not nothing,*
> *So that you can be totally in me.*

REFLECTION QUESTIONS

Am I aware of a desire in myself to be completely united to God in love? Do I recognize that God's desire for this relationship is immense and overwhelming? If this is something that both God and I desire, what could possibly hinder this union? What obstacles are there in my life that must be overcome before this union can proceed? How might changes in my daily habits affect this union for better or for worse? Am I willing to make more time for God in my life?

DAY TEN

God Changes Our Heart

—

FOCUS POINT

Faith, without good works, is dead. Christ is the Word, yes, but a word to be lived in us. A word that takes root in our souls, in our lives, and a word upon which we act in love. Our souls must be filled with the safety and surety of Christ, not the concerns and worries that the world provides. Our souls must be soft rather than hard, prepared to bend to the will of God and adhere to his divine plan. We must be bonded to God with hearts of flesh (not hearts of stone), for there is ultimate freedom in this love.

—

Man has a hard heart, he's stubborn, the prophets said and repeated it. Many proclaimed that God would change man's heart of stone into a heart of flesh, especially Jeremiah (31:31–34). Tauler has left us a sermon about Christ's words of reproach to his apostles about the hardness of their hearts:

> The disciples were sitting together and our Lord appeared to them and reproached them for their disbelief and the hardness of their hearts (S 18, 1; see Mk 16:14).

This teaching of God is eternal and echoes again, even today:

> Our Lord still inflicts this blame every day and at all times, on all of mankind...because of their disbelief and the hardness of their hearts.... This is a challenge to us. This theme is addressed especially to religious (Ibid).

Tauler appears to be stern. We do not lose our faith in an instant: however, it could fade. More often than not we keep our faith inert, without any influence on our behavior. Saint James wrote in his letter, "So faith by itself, if it has no works, is dead" (2:17); Saint Augustine continues: "It is not a true faith if it does not go to God with living charity and works."

Far from linking salvation to our actions, those authors recognize the vital appearance of our faith in daily life. The Resurrection of Christ changes our mentality; Christ presents himself to us as a truth to be believed, a dogma to be proclaimed, as a living being amongst us whose presence is equally felt by those who need our help as well as those who we consider to be our enemies. For the believer, each person is a vision of faith that transforms life!

Do we accept the following reproach regarding our lack of faith?

"If they recognized their guilt, they could be saved."

Nobody gets healed unless they recognize that they are sick; our pride keeps us from admitting that we are ill, to our detriment. In the Gospel, all healing is preceded by the words, "Son of David, have pity on me," or a similar request. We find a reminder of this in Psalm 94 (95): "...O that today you would listen to his voice. Do not harden your hearts, as at Meribah, as on the day at Massah in the wilderness, when your ancestors tested me and put me to the proof..." (7–9).

It is in the prophesies of Jeremiah that Tauler draws the most poignant expression of his reproach: "...they have forsaken me, the fountain of living water, and dug out cisterns for themselves, cracked cisterns that can hold no water" (Jer 2:13). This parable pleased Tauler for it indirectly makes reference to the depth: the bottom (depth) of a cistern is hard because of the stone, brick or cement there, while that of a spring is soft-light sand or clay. The first bottom, made by the hand of man, has limitations and may have defects; the second is of God's creation.

It is this way with the exterior and the interior soul. The cistern heart is filled with the world, the spring-soul with Christ. The Word is born at each moment in the living water and the life of each Christian is disrupted by the Holy

Spirit. The stagnant water of the cistern symbolizes arrogance, the harshness of judgments, hurtful words, while the spring water is a sign for humility, submission to God, obedience to the Lord, and fraternal rectification in the greatest of charity. The condemned sin is that of preferring the living water of the spring to the stagnant one of the cistern, to the life of the trinitarian God in us to our own sufficiency.

Tauler warns us against this mistake:

> Come on, true cisterns that you are! If the fountain of living water had ever sprung in your dry bottom (depth), never would we have found such a preferential group of persons, but instead, true, divine charity would flow from your depth! There would be neither blame nor shame, no severity of judgment, nor hardness of heart. All of this corruption ferments in the cisterns (S 18, 2).

The theme of the cistern unites with that of the hardness of the heart. The opposite of charity, this fault is serious because it is at the source of many sins: rash judgments, scandalmongering, and slander originate from it. The comparison of the cistern to the spring corresponds to that of the heart of stone to the heart of flesh, symbolized by equal charity towards all. Man is as changing as God is stable; divine, universal mercy is opposite to our preference for people. God frees us from our captivities which strangle us and restrain our spiritual blossoming. He frees us from the world, from the fracas of our meaningless upheavals, from inordinate love of ourselves, from our arrogance, and from our attachments to what we believe to be God and which is a misleading perception. Such is the action of the Word of God that is being born in us, transforming our depth of stone into a heart of flesh and making the Holy Spirit superabundantly flow from it. Therefore, here is Tauler's recommendation:

> Beware of your depth!
> My children, beware, I beg you, for the love of God, pay attention to your depth; beware of what preoccupies you; be soft and humble and submit yourself to God... (S 18, 3).

Beware of your depth, then, signifies the attention we must pay to that which enters or leaves us, the evil of the world, or the Word of God.

> It is by four spiritual operations, successive or simultaneous, that the Holy Spirit transforms our depth. First, it must destroy our hard depth, pulverize it, which does not happen without suffering (Ibid).

Tauler speaks about wounded love and wounding love:

> The soul is wounded by the rays of God's love, so that it may receive the living water of true charity, and in turn it hurts God with its love (S 18, 4).

The first of these wounds does not surprise us at all for if we lean towards God it is because he, himself, called us first. The second surprises us more: could man then injure

God other than by sin, wound him in love? Maybe Teresa of Ávila or John of the Cross, but us? The love of God never stops surprising us; instinctively we see it the same as our own: very restrained. From Christ's wounded open side on the cross flowed water and blood; a wound caused by a sword, by the sins of the world, by the love of God...that is true. But is it not also by the love of the saints (and of all people) who replied as well as they could, in love, to God's love?

Love is imprisoning:

> The prisoner of love is no longer the master of his thoughts or of his work, for he must abandon himself completely to the Beloved and to his love (S 18, 4).

Man knows the bonds of marriage as well as those of religious profession and the priesthood. Sad is the one who is alone and misunderstands the connection of love. Far from being a constraint or an enslavement, which is only a false philosophy of freedom, this bond, paradoxically, frees man. Jesus, in total freedom, bound himself to the will of his Father, and Mary, to that of God, each witnessing to a great love.

Tauler also speaks about the love of desire by purifying the expression of its carnal meaning that would be incompatible with God. The evolution of our love for God brings about an important phase of desire. If God is the one who is transcendent, he will also be unreachable and we could not desire him; if he was solely the All-Near, then possession of him would supersede all desire. Yet he is both, continuous absence and presence. The desire and the presence of the absent; and God is infinitely desirable.

Love consumes...this theme does not appear to be compatible with the one of the living water! And yet the love of God is a consuming fire and "a river that could not be crossed" (Ezek 47:5). The disaster is the same whether it is due to water or fire (or the two of them). May the fire of the Holy Spirit consume us or the living water submerge us, or the old man (Saint Paul) or the exterior man (Tauler) must disappear in favor of the interior man in which the Word of God is born.

> *May we then leave all of the cisterns*
> *So that the living water of charity*
> *Is poured into us.*

REFLECTION QUESTIONS

How does my faith manifest itself in my life? Do I belong to any organizations that suit my desire to serve? If not, and if I'm interested in serving with a group, where might I look to find out about such groups? Am I inspired to share my faith and God's love with the people I encounter in my life? With family and friends? With strangers? Am I aware of "evangelization moments" when they make themselves apparent in my life? Do I feel freer (from fear) when I am bonded to God in love? What are some of my natural expressions of the love I feel from God?

From Vigilance to Contemplation

FOCUS POINT

We must be vigilant and make certain that no weeds find a home in the field that is the soul. We must never be lax, believing that the pursuit of God is over, that we possess him. We do not possess God; he gives himself freely to us. And we never know him entirely, so our pursuit and opening up to him should never cease. We must contemplate God in his glory and live in this world simultaneously. God fills us with charity when we glance at him contemplatively, and we return to the world charged with his goodness and grace.

Just as in a single glance I gaze over all of you here, seated before me, everything is embraced with a single glance in the same abyss, in the same furnace of love, just as did the contemplatives. Then they carry their glances into the abyss of love, into the furnace of love, and rest there. Then, this ardent flame fell like a dew, over all those who, in holy Christianity, needed it, so that, soon they may return to the divine abyss and the loving rest of the silent shadows (S 24, 7).

S uch a contemplation constitutes the end of a long process; of a combat with ourselves and the victory won by Christ. In fact, the text is drawn from the end of the Twenty-Fourth Sermon which was dedicated to the preparation of the soul for the outpouring of the Holy Spirit at the Pentecost.

Tauler compares the Christian to a laborer and the soul to a field; just as the laborer pulls the weeds, tills the soil, and digs into it deeply, in the same way, the spiritual person should eradicate the harmful tendencies in the soul and verify its affections. Through conversion, it detaches itself from that which has been created and looks to God. Tauler prefers to speak about *digging into oneself* or *looking into one's own depth* in order to see the spring blossoming with the coming of the Holy Spirit.

The blossoming of the Holy Spirit is often preceded by sensory graces, ordinary or extraordinary; with them comes the question of how to welcome and use them. Tauler warns us against any abuse and shows us God's plan.

But when they feel, within themselves, this great and
extraordinary consolation and sweetness, some are
tempted to delve into it and just stay there, in that
enjoyment (S 24, 4).

In the eyes of many Christians, the Sunday liturgy, for example, is an obligation that they would willingly do without and daily prayer is a chore that they can barely suffer.
Then, one day, when they have a better understanding of
the celebrations of the mysteries, when prayer seems to touch
someone who is invisible but near, for them, God becomes
present. Their life takes on a new meaning.... It becomes
evident that God exists and loves them. Nothing is left to
be proved—all is evident.

Saint Peter fell into the trap. He felt comfortable on the
mount of the Transfiguration, just contemplating Moses,
Elijah, and Jesus. He would have liked to just stay there.
His mistake, which is also ours, was to stop the course of
things, to believe that the race was over, that he had seized
God! But God cannot be seized!

Those who fall into that trap are left behind and we
can expect nothing from them. Their progress is
stopped (S 24, 4).

In Tauler's mind there's no doubt that, in such a case, there
is a blockage in the spiritual life since we believe we have
reached our goal. That's the temptation of humanity: to
have a hold on God and appropriate him. But is that such a
great sin? God said: "Happy are the pure, for they shall see
God." Then why not just stop at that level of possession of

God? We can notice two errors: God is not conquered, he gives himself; if he has offered himself, it is seldom how and where we expect it.

Tauler uses the example of the apostles. They could see Christ much better than we could, for he lived amongst them in all his goodness, mercy, and miracles.... So what more could they want? Jesus told them: "it is to your advantage that I go away, for if I do not go away, the Advocate will not come to you; but if I go, I will send him to you" (Jn 16:7).

There is a lesson in the purification of the apostles' hearts: always reach higher. "[W]hat we have seen with our eyes, what we have looked at and touched with our hands...we testify to it" (1 Jn 1:1–2). John can only proclaim the Word because he has stopped seeking the pre-Easter Jesus. He has stopped looking at Jesus in his human nature in order to identify him with the Word of God: "In the beginning was the Word, and the Word was with God, and the Word was God" (Jn 1:1). Through the Incarnation, eternity penetrated into our finite time temporarily. So God's favors, which are not God himself but a visible manifestation of his presence, can only be temporary. The danger is to consider them as definite and to not go any further.

When, in his Twenty-Fourth Sermon, Tauler says "they fall into a false freedom," he warns that it is a mistake to stop seeking God. He sees Christian freedom as a complete adhesion to good without any constraints, either internal or external.

We will be surprised by the following from Tauler:

Must we flee that sweetness and push it away? No, in no way. We must, however, accept it with much gratefulness and return it to God with humility (S 24, 5).

We are far from Jansen's theory of a nature to be destroyed. Tauler is moderate in his asceticism. Instead of refusing God's gifts, he prefers to accept them with humility, gratitude, and thanksgiving. Before being able to love your neighbor as yourself, you must first love yourself. So, refusing God's gifts would be to underestimate ourselves and others while God's love includes all of our brothers.

Rather than stopping to search for God through excessive complacency with his gifts, Tauler proposes to remain active:

Beloved children, do not be lethargic and passive, do not rest in anything that is not purely God. Maintain an ongoing self-examination, in the light of the virtue of discretion, and, in a desire that is filled with love, remain attentive to yourself and God within you (S 24, 5).

Arrogance makes us reject the sensory grace, while discretion makes us use it judiciously without abuse. Tauler summarizes the attitude that we must adopt:

It must excite the desire of his heart and the flame of his love even more (Ibid).

Where your heart is, there you will also find your treasure. Let it be in God. As for the flame of his love, it introduces us to the gifts of the Holy Spirit. Thus, vigilance leads to contemplation.

It has often been said about contemplative life that it is passive and ignores the reality of the world. Tauler refutes that criticism by showing that there is no real contemplation of God unless it is followed by a glance upon the world. There is no thanksgiving unless it is supported by intercession. The contemplative glance lifts itself from the world to God and, from him, returns to Christianity only to better return to God. Man, living between finite time and eternity, looks, in turn, to the creator and to his creation. The glance of the contemplative is deemed to be an abyss as well as a furnace of love:

> Thus, they embrace everything in one glance (in the same abyss, furnace of love) (Ibid).

In the metaphor of the fire, which is dear to Tauler and Meister Eckhart, fire transforms the wood into more fire; here, God, also called the abyss of love, the furnace of love, transforms the contemplative's glance into charity, which is also called love and mercy. God sees the world with mercy and also gives that same glance to the friend of God (the contemplative).

Tauler's God is a God of love whose Holy Spirit of love unites the Father and the Son. The friend of God casts his glance from the world to the Father and from him to the world by flow and reflux. Tauler sees, in God, a flow that starts from the unity of the divine essence, the origin of everything, which crosses the profound and fertile nature of God and constitutes the nature of the Father, Son, and

Holy Spirit. This flow goes from God to the multitude. Inversely, the Son returns to the Father by a reflux of the eternal generation towards the one from whom it originates. In the extra-trinitarian flow, the Word of God became man and dwelled amongst us so that he could lead humanity to God in his reflux: Jesus said, "I am going to the Father," but it is with us that he returned. The glance of the friend of God enters into this flow and reflux of the Word. Cast upon God, this glance is a resting place, for God is one and the oneness could only be a resting place; but cast upon the world, it becomes dynamic, for the needs of holy Christianity are many. Lord, make us become contemplatives.

May we all become like
Those noble people,
useful to all Christians:
Who serve to help to better mankind
For the glory of God
And the consolation of all... (see S 24, 7).

REFLECTION QUESTIONS

Do I ever feel satisfied with my relationship with God? How can I overcome these moments of laxity in my spiritual life? Are there new ways to pursue God; new avenues by which I can open myself to him in contemplation so that he might fill me with his charity? How attentive am I to the weeds that appear in my soul? Can I recognize a pattern of behavior in my life that allows these weeds to take root? How do I go about addressing/reversing this pattern?

DAY TWELVE

The Image of the Invisible God

FOCUS POINT

God's mercy and love for us is great. He seeks us at every turn, at every moment, because his love for us is so great. The Father sent his Son to us so that mankind would be restored to excellence, to a union with the Divine. God sought us in the darkness and he found us there, cold and afraid. He comforts us through his Son and energizes us by his Holy Spirit. We need only look into the depths of our soul to see the image of the invisible God imprinted upon us. We have been claimed for God by God.

Let God act in us, break the hardness of our heart, and defeat our refusal. That is neither a resignation, nor a rest, but a clear understanding that the work to be done surpasses our strength, that only God could realize it, and that we must, in no way, hinder his action.

The sanctification is the restoration of the image of God into the depth of the soul which had been destroyed by sin. In order to describe this rebuilding, Tauler calls on a parable from the Gospel: the parable of the lost coin (Lk 15:8–10). If we stray a bit from its original meaning, we can compare God's mercy in seeking lost humanity to the poor woman who returns to her home to seek a lost piece of money with the help of a lamp. Tauler highlights another meaning that is perhaps secondary but, all the same, real: just as the coin has the effigy of the emperor, the soul carries the image of God.

> The soul's effigy should be clear; it is not enough for this effigy to be an imitation of God, it must be God's image, his pure and divine essence. And then, here, in this image, God loves himself, knows himself, and rejoices in himself. He lives and acts in it. Here the soul becomes clearly like God, exactly the same as God, divine. Through grace, it becomes all that God is by his nature, closely united with God; plunged into God, it is elevated in God above itself (S 37, 5).

In the parable of the woman and the lost coin, this woman symbolizes God's mercy, the lit lamp Christ's humanity, and the lost coin humanity that is separated from God. The upset of the household shows the wound in God's heart, his mercy, and condescension. But what was most important to our preacher was the effigy on the piece of money.

A coin is struck from a seal or a die, a negative that imprints its design upon it. What is the divine die that marks each soul and transfers its image upon it? Man was created in the image and likeness of God; Tauler, like many other spiritual masters, saw, in this image, the capacity of man to know and love God. The perceived intelligence and effectiveness of man, then, constitutes the image of God in the heart of everyone.

Sin caused problems with and clouded this image and it must be restored. God "in the fullness of time," sent his Son amongst us, to dwell with us, in order to restore the image within us that had been destroyed and to give it an even closer resemblance. That is God's bounty: man destroys, God restores.

Now, it is not only in creation alone that man seeks and discovers God, but in his own "depth," in his "noble depth." He sees his abilities multiply, his field of performance increase to unsuspecting dimensions. Able to discern God externally, he finds himself able to grasp him more profoundly "internally." What happened? The image of God, Christ, visited man and reestablished his image and likeness.

It is written, with reference to Jesus: "He is the image of the invisible God, the firstborn of all creation..." (Col 1:15); "For those whom he foreknew he also predestined to be conformed to the image of his Son, in order that he might be the firstborn within a large family" (Rom 8:29). Therefore, Christ is the perfect image of his Father and, by his coming, he restored and reestablished the image of God in us. The Incarnation, limited strictly in time to a few decades, finds its prolongation into the centuries. We can now go back to Tauler's first text and be amazed at it with him: "It is not enough that the soul is an imitation of God...." That is a reminder of man's original condition, of his abilities and his grandeur as well as his limitations. Christ came and he "marked us with the imprint of the Holy Spirit," in a new effigy.

> But this effigy is the same image as God himself, his
> pure and divine essence... (Ibid).

The Word is the true image of God and his divine essence. Tauler believed that the effigy of God in man is the image of the invisible God. Although the die imprinted in wax can cool, it cannot be that way for the spiritual reality that it represents. For the Word of God could not cool and only leaves a soul when he is chased out by major sins; otherwise, he is alive and dwells infinitely in the soul. He acts in the soul. That presupposes that he was born in the soul. In Tauler's mind, that birth of God corresponds to the effigy on the coin. The image is born at the time of baptism and is renewed by the sacraments.

He is alive in the soul, for Jesus is essentially life itself, just as he is the way and the truth and just as God is a living God and the God of the living. Just as the die imprints the shape, the Holy Spirit gives life, eternal and divine life.

Jesus dwells in the soul, Tauler continues, as he echoes at the same time Saint John, who teaches us that: "And the Word became flesh and lived among us" (Jn 1:14), and Jesus' words: "Just as you, Father, are in me and I am in you, may they also be in us…may they be one as we are one…me in them, and you in me" (Jn 17:21a, 22, 26). The unity of the Word and the believer is paralleled to that of the Father and the Son.

Jesus acts in the soul and, through this action of God, Tauler sees God's work: in this image, God loves himself, he recognizes himself and rejoices in himself. He repeats what he does in the Holy Trinity in the soul of the believer, in his depth: that is, his act of love, of knowledge, and generation. In the depth of our soul, God engenders God, the Father engenders the Son. That is where we find the origin of Tauler's first sermon about the Nativity:

> The third birth is the one by which God, every day
> and at all times, is truly born spiritually by grace
> and love into a good soul (S 1, 1).

God engenders his Son in the believer's soul: light born of the light, God born of the true God.

The birth of the Word and his presence in the soul transforms it by an extremely deep mutation that completely changes its nature. "Here, the soul becomes a total resemblance of God, divine" (Ibid).

It is a true metamorphosis, as the soul goes from being human to being divine.

If it is not God, at least it receives the divine nature of the Trinity. Its nature becomes totally transformed, elevated from its natural human condition to a divine one, it becomes a likeness of God. Not only does the image of the invisible God restore the original image in our depth, it also replaces it. Through grace, the soul becomes everything that God is by nature and we become sons in the Son, receiving his divine nature, we are heirs of the divine life with and in the sole Heir. The Father engenders us with his Son, he by nature, us through mercy and grace.

It is difficult for us to grasp God's gift, to conceive of that deification or its depth, which is offered to us and to which we are called—and for eternity as well. A contemporary Jewish mystic says: "It is easier for us to believe in the wrath of God than in his mercy, for wrath is a feeling that is very human, while mercy is divine." God's gift is almost unbelievable and our faith dares not accept it.

May we achieve that simple yet great union, not a fusion, for God remains God and every one of us retains his own personality, but profound union in which the separation of persons, divine and human, cannot hinder the gift and the sharing of the divine nature.

May God and the soul become one!

REFLECTION QUESTIONS

Do I sense God seeking me out in the darker corners of my life, like the woman searching for her lost coin? What is my response to this mercy and love? I have not earned this mercy and love, yet God gives it to me. How can I express my gratitude to him for all he gives to me? Can I perhaps attempt to recognize his image imprinted upon my soul, and live my life in accordance with the divine reality that surrounds me and is united to me in the deepest part of my person?

DAY THIRTEEN

Three Qualities of Love

FOCUS POINT

God is love and the soul in which he dwells becomes love. As we grow in God we grow in love. Tauler identifies three stages in the growth of love: soft love, in which there is a focus on the Incarnation, the recognition of Jesus Christ within each one of us; wise love, where there is a focus on the eternal nature of the Divine (and detachment from those things that are less than God); and strong love, which centers on the need for humility in the face of God's pure love.

What is left to man who is deified, made in the image of God? He has a soul filled with God and a body inflicted with suffering. But then God's glance enters the depth of that soul like a lightning bolt so often that any suffering appears to become too small. And that sudden burst of God into the very depth of that soul makes it see, in a flash, what it must do (S 57, 8).

A t the day of his baptism, man becomes deified, he is filled with divine grace, but every day he still has to become what he is: the son of God. This growing filial relationship is only equaled by the increase of our charity. Just as Saint Bernard did, Tauler sees three stages in the growth of charity. It would be fruitless to try and describe them precisely: man, like faith, is a plant that keeps growing even though, at times, he seems to reach thresholds, slows down, or accelerates. Love is at work; strong love, wise love, crisscrossing one another, existing and growing together. However, experience shows that it is justified to make this distinction: only strong love cannot be overtaken by temptation (see Song 7). Tauler substitutes his own terminology for that of Saint Bernard: he speaks of internal, external, and essential love.

Before tackling the subject of love, Tauler warns us of its subterfuges which sometimes lead more to arrogance than to charity:

We often aim for arrogance (pride), honor, one's own advantage, to be well-known and held in high esteem. In short, everything that man does in order to elevate himself, to make himself look better...and gain the esteem of others (S 52, 2).

That vainglory nips in the bud any attempt to find true love. A false love of God that rests on self-contentment, the search for God as the source of an overestimated intellectual satisfaction, leads to a dead end. Tauler says: "Joy and the feeling of spiritual well-being brought by devotion" (S 52, 2) constitute an important obstacle to the development of love in us, because they make us mistake the road for the goal. By avoiding those gross errors, we have access to the true road to love.

> God uses kindness to attract man and incite him to
> go forward in order that, through God's feeling, true
> love will be born and grow (S 52, 3).

Here, love is healthy and holy. It is desired by God and we can use it in as much as God wants us to. We can't reach God if we delve into the joy of the spiritual journey—that is not an end, it is a means to that end. God's gifts are not God. Contrary to other more austere authors, Tauler counsels us:

> To not reject that grace, but to receive it with rever-
> ence and humility, attributing its smallness and low
> personal value to the fact that God has to attract us
> and incite us in this manner (S 52, 3).

Being a wise spiritual guide, Tauler prefers humility to asceticism; his poor health led him to this conclusion.

Soft love encourages us to pass from external sensory practices to more interior ones. Human nature is such that man must draw from external experiences in order to internalize and acquire intellectual knowledge of the abstract. There is no knowledge of God except through his Word, and, in turn, it is only understood through his Incarnation. Jesus tells us who he and his Father are: whoever sees me, sees my Father. Tauler qualifies this first love of God as "sweet, sensitive, and imaginative" (S 52, 3), for it is based upon images perceived by the senses, of which the cross and holy images are the most known.

> Then follows the second love described by Saint Bernard, which he calls wise love, that is, reasonable love. Children, this love is much higher and elevated than the first...the noble and wise love of reason is something noble, precious, and delectable...you must apply your fundamental will to eternal things...to what lies inside, to the eternal birth (S 52, 4).

Tauler brings us back to our main subject: we cannot stall ourselves at the contemplation of Jesus, born of Mary in Bethlehem. Beyond that birth, we must see the birth of God, who has come to visit his own and live amongst them. Here, nothing is left to the senses. Looking at the Virgin's infant, some believe and adore him, others refuse and are upset. More than a love of reason, the love that appears is one of faith, built on the revelation: Eckhart's noble love. Tauler defines it as:

> You must apply your fundamental will to eternal things (Ibid).

Through the teachings of John of the Cross and Meister Eckhart, both great spiritual masters, Tauler has developed his own views about noble love. He believes that spiritual difficulties favor the growth of love, they strengthen it and transform sweet love into strong love.

> Strong love is the true love in which the Lord is present: he shines so brightly in the depth of the soul that the spirit (mind), in consequence of its human weakness, cannot endure it and must necessarily faint and be rejected in its powerlessness. Then the mind has no support and all it has left is to throw itself into the divine abyss and lose itself in it so that it knows nothing on its own... (S 52, 6).

Out of this description of strong love, we draw five aspects:

- The Lord is present in strong love and that presence is the third birth of the Word. The Trinity is present in us in its eternal act of generation, love, and being;
- God illuminates the very depth of the soul. The divine presence is, at the same time, light and barely perceptible, a hurricane and an ardent fire. The light acquired by faith can be followed by

the light of intelligence and wisdom. God's en-
lightenments are diverse, the most intense remain
impossible to be explained by the mystics;

- The ways of God are not ours and his light can
  only throw our mind into a state of power-
  lessness…and the mind can only throw itself into
  and drown in the divine abyss. Abandonment is
  required because the one who relies on his own
  strengths cannot count on God;

- God essentially illuminates the very depth of the
  soul. The word "essentially" denotes the oneness
  of God's action, the infused knowledge which is
  given, as opposed to human knowledge;

- Finally, the invitation to throw oneself into and
  drown in the divine abyss evokes our baptism,
  the initial immersion into God, into the death and
  resurrection of Christ, the primary source of divine life. If, at baptism, we are immersed into the
  Easter mystery, in this case, we are immersed in
  the indwelling of God within us into the mystery
  of the trinitarian life in our soul.

Oh abyss of God's wealth, wisdom,
And knowledge,
Charity never ends.
Faith, hope, and charity remain,
But the greatest of these
Is charity (see 1 Cor 13:8, 13).

REFLECTION QUESTIONS

Can I identify the three qualities of love outlined by Tauler in my own life? Do I have a tendency to stall in my spiritual life, afraid or lax to pursue God to newer and deeper levels of spirituality? Do I see the need for humility in my spiritual pursuits? That I must never confuse the path for the goal? That I must always be willing to abandon a previous (and comfortable) means of pursuing God when a newer, more effective, and/or frightening path presents itself?

DAY FOURTEEN

The Glory of the Father

FOCUS POINT

We are all called to greater holiness in our lives. We are
called to grow in love in the glory of God. Jesus Christ calls
us in three ways, says Tauler. We are called to leave the
external world and enter into the internal depths of the soul,
detaching ourselves from the attachments that tempt us.
We are called to contemplate Jesus Christ in our soul and
live with the nourishment that unity provides. Finally, we
are called to receive the Holy Spirit into our lives and allow
the power of the Spirit to move our lives in the love of God
and neighbor. We must be patient in all of this, though, for
holiness is a lifelong pursuit.

How could man understand the union with God? Those who achieve that state act outside of time, in eternity, outside of what is created, in what is uncreated, outside of multiplicity into simplicity. In the midst of confusion, they have peace and dig, with loving desire, into the depth, attributing all good things to God because they are eternally in him and he keeps them in his love and thoughts (S 15, 3).

———

The growth of love is linked with the birth of the Word of God, and it allows us to participate, to a certain extent, during our life on earth, in the glory of the Word next to the Father. The Christ that is born in our soul is the same one that rose from the dead on Easter morning, he is the one who is seated at the right of the Father in glory. He prayed so that his glory would rain down on humanity: "So now, Father, glorify me in your own presence with the glory that I had in your presence before the world existed. (...) The glory that you have given me, I have given them..." (Jn 17:5, 22).

Let's look at Jesus' prayer to his Father which reminds us that we are in him. On the eve of his passion, redemption seems to have been accomplished, as if he had already lived his agony. Tauler says that he was "speaking from the point of view of eternity" (S 15, 2), showing that, to some extent, our resurrection and glorification were already fulfilled.

Prayer is an elevation towards God, it sets out from a concrete life situation and goes up to the Father, an ascending motion, but also one of interiorization, for the soul who lifts itself to God also descends into itself in a moment of spiritualization and simplification. From the multiplicity of words, the soul liberates itself and turns towards the unity of contemplation. The spoken prayer is the basis of the mental prayer which becomes contemplation under the action of grace. In this spiritualization, the soul relies upon God and is moved by the Holy Spirit who accomplishes, in our world, its sanctification. A man amongst men, Jesus includes in his prayers all the prayers of humanity, past, present, and to come. Our prayers become one with his, which is the prayer of God-made-man.

God doesn't impose his gifts on us but proposes them; not all at once, but spread across time. This first glorification, since we are still in a valley of tears, God offers to us in three successive stages. Tauler deals briefly on the similarities of these to Jesus' three calls to John:

- The first call to John was to leave the world in order to follow Christ. Even if Tauler was speaking to religious, it can have significance for us: more generally, to leave the external self and turn to the internal, purifying our affections.
- The second call invited John to rest on the heart of Jesus. For us, Tauler proposes that we contemplate upon Christ in our soul in order to grasp the difference which exists and separates these two depths: just how different we are from this model and small we are. This second call is a eucharistic one. For Tauler asks us to compare our image to that of Christ present in the Eucharist, especially regarding charity, humility, and tenderness. Christ

expressed the greatest of each of these qualities in order to give himself to all mankind through this sacrament. He is our spiritual nourishment. God glorifies man through prayer, removes him from a world filled from sin, and transplants man into his kingdom. He feeds them with the body and the blood of his beloved Son.

• On the third call, John received the Holy Spirit. Jesus opened the door to heaven and led John through it. God is the master of when these doors open and close for us.

Tauler has difficulty in explaining the inexplicable. Implicitly, he sends us to the fourth Gospel. Because he had been called by Jesus, rested his head on his Master, and received the Holy Spirit, John was to write these disturbing pages. For us, we could never hope to give a witness of such magnitude, but each of us can according to the degree in which we have been called, where we have contemplated him in the Eucharist. The Holy Spirit has kept the door open for us.

Even though it is noble and great, the program is nonetheless arduous. Everything takes time, even holiness.

> *Do not be afraid;*
> *This does not happen in one day*
> *or one year.*
> *It requires simplicity,*
> *Purity, abandonment.*
> *Such is the way, the most perfect of all,*
> *That is given to you and I*
> *By the Father, Son, and the Holy Spirit.*

REFLECTION QUESTIONS

How do I respond to the three calls Tauler mentions above? Am I able to turn away from the external and detach myself from those things that are less than God? Am I able to contemplate Christ in my soul and unite my will to his? Am I willing to accept the Holy Spirit into my life and be guided in love by the grace of God? Am I patient with all of this spiritual growth? Do I recognize that holiness is a journey, a lifelong path of love for God and neighbor?

DAY FIFTEEN

Filled With the Holy Spirit

FOCUS POINT

The Holy Spirit is called the Sanctifier; he makes us participants in the sanctification of God. It is also through the Holy Spirit that we will end our meditation, asking him to grant us what God expects of us: to become saints. At work in the early Church and throughout the centuries, the Holy Spirit has kept the Church holy and without sin. The Holy Spirit continues to guide the Church as a whole and its people individually. Our openness to the Spirit allows for greater growth in the love of God.

The disciples were all filled with the Holy Spirit. One must take note here of the disciples' disposition, at that time, when this occurred; it is the one that each of us must have. They were assembled, behind closed doors, and quietly seated when the Holy Spirit was sent to them. The Holy Spirit is sent to each person every time they turn away from creations and turn to God. At the very instant that a person does that, the Holy Spirit comes with his list of gifts and fills the depth of that soul completely (S 26, 2).

The preparation of the soul for the introduction of the Holy Spirit requires many of the things we have already spoken about, but we will briefly recap them here. On the tenth day, Tauler recommended that we become laborers in the field of our soul, weeding out the capital sins, and achieve peace with God. This remote condition having been fulfilled, or at least somewhat, we come to:

> the next preparation, the most true that we can do in order to receive the Holy Spirit, to truly receive him without an intermediary and in grand fashion. That is: true detachment, passivity, the internal spirit, and unification (S 23, 2).

In Tauler's eyes, passivity is the affirmation of God's sovereignty and the recognition that he, alone, is the Master of all sanctification. With respect to the interior life, we already know that it constitutes Tauler's main theme.

The realization of those conditions determines our capacity to receive God. Everything must contribute to the increase of this capacity for God. The Holy Spirit prepares us for his own coming.

We already know what attitude Tauler recommends for this coming: humility, thanksgiving, and, at the same time, acceptance and distance with respect to spiritual consolations. The enjoyment of God's gifts is not God. Do not stop at his gifts, for they are not the goal.

Tauler also speaks of Christian freedom, which he sees as the power to freely choose whether or not to accept to do God's will; it would seem that this gift of the Holy Spirit liberates us just as the Transfiguration freed the apostles. We must remember that this freedom is very fragile.

Tauler incessantly warns us of the danger of giving in to the feeling that we have "made it," thus letting down our defenses against Satan and "slacking off" our progress on the spiritual path to God. Satan knows all of our weaknesses and plays on them, offering us false rewards.

The last temptation of the seeker of God is to attach himself more to the sensory feeling of the joy of God's presence than to God himself. It is subtle, real, and dangerous. If that feeling is not God, where can we find him?

The Eucharist, the body of Christ, is broken and shared with all Christians. It constitutes the privileged place to meet God. Jesus said that he would be with us until the end of time; this, he fulfills in the Eucharist. The growing body of the Church is also another proof of God's presence.

Finally, it is in fraternal charity that we can best join in the love of Christ: the love of God and of man having become the one and only love.

Although the seeker of God is likely to encounter some

deceptions (temptations), he must not attribute them to God. They purify him and lead him to a genuine spiritual experience. In spite of our vigilance, our perception of God remains personal and God may "escape" us.

The All-Other transcends the world and ideas. He comes to the level of our world; he didn't lift himself up, but descended to us! We think he is rich and he came to us as one of the most poor; we seek the creator of the world and are spoken to about the humility of God. In order to find God "very low," that is where he descended, to our world, we must elevate ourselves "very high."

Mentioning the faculty of reason, Tauler speaks of the intelligence illuminated by faith, the revelation moved by the Holy Spirit. The reception of the Holy Spirit "in a way that is more noble and more delightful" signifies the play between the supernatural virtues and the gifts of the Holy Spirit. In order to arrive at the coming of the Holy Spirit and to his making a dwelling in us, we must open ourselves:

> In the interior depth, the mysterious depth of the spirit; and it is only here that this delight has its true and proper place. It is here that the Holy Spirit is truly received in reality, only here, in this austere place, where man awakens (S 24, 6).

In order to speak about the life in the Holy Spirit, Tauler uses the term "awaken": man awakens. That reminds us of Christ's awakening (resurrection) from the dead through the power of the Holy Spirit. It connects the life in the Holy Spirit to Jesus' resurrection. Tauler says that the Holy Spirit is truly received in reality. That refers to the true path that was opened by Christ in his Father's kingdom: Jesus is the truth and the life. Jesus is both real and divine. It appears to be a paradox, yet it is not. Jesus came to man in order to restore God's image in his depth.

God lives in silence and retreat:

> The more man devotes himself, hour after hour, to his movement of retreat, the more he will be conscious of this interior and ever-growing manifestation of the Holy Spirit which had been given to him right from the beginning (S 26, 2).

At the end of our reflection on the birth of God in us, let us be conscious of the eternal aspect of this truth. Blessed Sister Elizabeth of the Trinity told us nothing but this fact: pay attention to the three divine Persons who live within you. Tauler stresses the person of the Word, Elizabeth stresses the Trinity. The aspect of the birth of the Word, strongly underlined by Tauler, is replaced by Elizabeth's aspect of "habitation." In spite of these discrepancies, they do have a common theme: let us seek God within ourselves, at the very depth of our soul, founded on the same Gospel of Jesus Christ, transmitted either by John or Paul. "All of the disciples were filled with the Holy Spirit."

Come Holy Spirit!
Light the fire of your love in us.
Oh heavenly king, consoler, spirit of truth,
You who are present everywhere,
and who fill everything,
Treasure of wealth and giver of life,

Come and dwell in us,
Purify us of all stain,
And save our souls,
You who are all goodness.

REFLECTION QUESTIONS

Do I allow the Holy Spirit to energize me and guide me in my life? Am I open to the Spirit's goodness in my life? In what ways can I be more open to the Spirit? By dropping attachments that prevent my full attention from being given to the Spirit? Do I pray that the Holy Spirit—and the Trinity as a whole—will be at the center of my existence as I strive to serve God and live my life as a saint would, giving God all that I am at every moment of the day?

Bibliography

Ozment, S. E. *Homo Spiritualis: A Comparative Study of the Anthropology of Johannes Tauler, Jean Gerson and Martin Luther*. Brill Academic Publishers, 1997.

Steiner, Rudolf. *Mystics of the Renaissance: Jacob Boehme, Meister Eckhart, Paracelsus, Giordano Bruno, Tauler*. Gordon Press, 1991.

Tauler, Johannes. *Sermons* (from the *Classics of Western Spirituality* series). Translated by Maria Shrady. Paulist Press, 1985.

———. *Signposts to Perfection: A Selection From the Sermons of Johann Tauler*. Edited and translated by Elizabeth Strakosch. B. Herder Book Company, 1958.

———. *Spiritual Conferences*. Edited and translated by Eric Colledge and Sister Jane, O.P. B. Herder Book Company, 1961.